Don`t Delay Writing You Book

Paperback ISBN 978-0-6480789-9-9
eBook ISBN 978-0-6483653-0-3

Aenghus Chisholme

Connect with Aenghus Chisholme:
www.aenghuschisholme.com

Cover by Andjela Vujic (Varvara11 on guru.com)

Also, by Aenghus Chisholme

Merlin the Sorcerer AD491

Guinevere the Queen AD494

Sir Gawain and the Green Knight AD499

Arthur the King AD517

Murder on the Mary Celeste

Jack the Ripper: The Murder of Madam Athalia

The Monster of Matlock

The Best Things in Life Begin with the Letter B

Buddy's Big Adventure

This book is dedicated to you, the reader that wants to be a writer; now is the time.

Table of Contents

Introduction

Thinking of writing a book but procrastinating? Well; by not writing it you are withholding your contribution to the bibliotheca of human literature. Seriously! You are depriving people out there in "reader-land" of a story that may inspire or touch them in a way that you had not planned and could not foresee.

So, really; you're just being selfish. It is time to shake off the shackles of procrastination that you have put on yourself and get to work. This book is all about how I have managed to hold down a full-time job. A gym regime. A social life and still I have produced eight books to date. This is my ninth. And I intend to go on and write a tenth, eleventh, twelfth and so on.

Whether or not you just want to tell one story, or you want to transform yourself from "someday I'll do it" to accomplished author with multiple books attributable to you; this book is for you!

***

I get scared before I write. It has happened before I have started every one of my books. I don't have any justifiable reason to base this fear upon. I can look at my bookshelf and see the past works that I have produced. I have had enough feedback from the readers to assure me that they are all enjoyable stories. However, that does not stop the encroaching fear of "what if.........." from trying to scuttle my endeavours.

Fear is a natural self-defence mechanism designed by mother nature to prevent you from doing anything to yourself that may be harmful. But in this case, it is not a protection mechanism at all. It is a sabotaging of your own right to put into words that story that you have been thinking about for so long.

"But what if it is no good?"

You can ask yourself a hundred questions that will erode your self-esteem and pick away at your confidence if you want. Go ahead do it now? Ask yourself every single question that best exemplifies your fears. They will probably include:

"I don't even know if I can write a book"

"I don't want anyone to read it and tell me that it is no good"

"I'm not a proper author"

"Who would want to read anything that I write anyway"

They are all subterfuge. Any one of them would be enough to put you off from writing. The group of them may send you scurrying away seeking safety. The safety of not writing.

The best exercise that I can give you to get over this hurdle is to have a book handy. A story that you have really enjoyed, by an author that you admire. Open the book to any random page and read one page only.

What you will see are simple sentence structures. Sentences making up paragraphs of ideas and themes. And by the end of the page nothing has changed. You are still seeing sentences and paragraphs. Not that remarkable really.

That author that you so admire, has written in simple prose, a story that is the sum of many very ordinary parts. And those ordinary parts can be done, over and over again, until they come together to form a cohesive book.

If that author that you like so much can do it. Guess what? You can do it too.

***

We all suffer from not having enough time to get done everything that we want to do. But it is up to you to prioritise this task up to the level that it deserves. Putting it off until you have more time is just doing you harm. If you don't do this now, you will always wonder if you could have achieved it. If you can follow the very simple steps that I have done in order to get myself to write, not once, but multiple times; you will succeed. They are in the following chapters. I will give you the steps leading up to and actually writing your book. Then there are the necessary steps that you must take in order to get it finished and then published.

We live in a wonderful world. Thanks to the advent of print-on-demand books and eBooks, anyone can self-publish their work. You can get it done and hold your book in your hands. Believe me, the sense of accomplishment and pride that you will have in your completed work is very intoxicating. It greatly eclipses any self-doubt or fear that I have had when it comes to writing. And looking at my current body of work, I am confident that I will continue to write books for the rest of my life.

Chapter 1: Step 1- Sacrifice

If time to write has been a problem up to now, then it is time to take away that blocker. We are all busy with our lives. Work-life; home-life, there don't seem to be enough hours in the day to get done what we would like to do. And that includes down-time. That is, time to just relax.

If like me, you have a hectic job and a daily commute and a rigid gym regime. Then by the time that you get home in the evening all you want to do is attempt to relax.

Wrong!

If you want to relax, save it for the weekend. I put to you, that you should be writing on the days that you work. If that is Monday to Friday, then I want you to put aside time after work Monday to Thursday to work. That way you will get into a rhythm of working in your job when you are there, and when you are at home, writing. It is a discipline like anything else. Why not Friday? Well, all work and no play will make you a dull person. Friday evening, Saturday and Sunday are when you can schedule your social, family and friends time.

It will take sacrifice. I used to be a big fan of the Simpsons cartoon on television. I like a good laugh. I would look forward to the new episodes when they were on and watch the re-runs when they were aired. But, in order to write, I turned my back on watching television in the evenings completely, Monday through Thursday. Not something that I ever thought that I would do; but I did it nevertheless. I simply needed that time to write instead of passively watch stories written by somebody else.

I replaced my passive way of relaxing, with an active way of relaxing. Instead of enjoying the characters and situations that somebody else had written, I began to create the characters and storylines that came directly out of my own imagination.

Ultimately, it is far more satisfying than any television program that I can watch. All of these years later, I can now barely sit and watch any amount of television. I get restless and begin to think that I should be doing something more creative. Something that achieves an end rather than merely viewing a show.

***

Look at how you are spending your time and work out what must be sacrificed in order for you to attain your goal of becoming an author. There is time that can be reclaimed from some habitual task that you would normally indulge in. What you need to do is to think of writing as more important than frittering-away your time with other pursuits.

I recall sitting in a community college out-of-hours course on creative writing back in the year 2010. I was one of about sixteen attendees. All of which wanted to write and none of which actually were.

We all had the same excuse. Exhausting days at work and thinking of spending time writing when we got home was a little off-putting. The reality is, that this was a huge wake-up call for me. I was one of many frustrated writers that was making excuses to myself on exactly why I wasn't writing.

I was cured by that class. I looked around at my classmates and thought

"I don't want to be like any of you; wanting to write but making excuses as to why I do not!"

I came home from those classes (I finished the ten-week course by the way, unlike about half of my compatriots), and set about writing. Step one in my plan was to MAKE the time to write. And not think of it as a chore. Problem solved. Simpsons, and indeed almost all television was immediately deleted from my evening schedule. And writing added to my evenings, as the way that I now actively relax and prefer to spend my time.

It's just like that time when I was 18 and decided to give up chocolate for some reason that is now obscured with the passing years. By week ten of not touching the stuff I had been transformed. I couldn't touch the chocolate for years after that. I didn't like the sight smell nor taste of it. Probably did me the world of good too.

But, I digress. If you make the sacrifice and create the time to write and do it over and over again, then it becomes part of your life. You will soon not be able to understand why you waited so long to do it.

What I want you to take away from this chapter is that when you are working, schedule your writing in-between. Save your relaxation for those days that you are not working. You will still need to maintain a social life; keep up with family and friends. Delegate your working days to the days that you write. Create the time for writing because it is very important. You will never get your book written unless you take it seriously enough to do this.

Work out now, exactly what you will need to sacrifice in order to make the time to write your book.

Chapter 2: Step 2 – Plan, Research & Overall Summary

If you fail to plan, then you plan to fail. That is how the old saying goes. And in the case of your novel it is absolutely true. It is all about the research that you need to do in order to make your story believable.

For example; before I wrote "Murder on the Mary Celeste" I had to research the boat itself. I learnt that it was a Brigantine class sailing vessel. I obtained a plan of the ship so that I knew its configuration. I researched the route that it took from New York through the Azores and supposedly onwards to Italy. Of course, it never reached Italy. It was found adrift off the Azores abandoned.

When I was in the planning stage of the Monster of Matlock, I researched how the towns looked in the late 1800's. I found everything that I could including original maps of the area so that I knew the topography of the townships. It was necessary for me to set the scene in my mind and then convey that to the reading audience. I found photographs of what the buildings looked like back in the year 1893. I saved pictures of the main ones and printed them out.

This planning phase however, can be a trap. And worse than that, it can become another excuse for you to not write.

Don't get too bogged-down in the research. In the business world it is called analysis-paralysis. Meaning, that you are so busy analysing and researching that you fail to get on with the business of running the show.

You have to draw a line in the sand at some point and conclude your research. Ensure that it does not take any longer than a week. If you are spending your Monday to Thursday writing, then four time periods should be enough for you to get together the necessary information about your overall setting that you need. It is a nice segue to the next step.

Print all of it out and begin to form a booklet of information about your story. Believe me, you will be referring to it throughout the writing process much more than you might think.

The result of this should not only be the main research that you need in order to get your book done and make it believable. But you should also come out of this step with an overall plot summary. It doesn't have to be too detailed at this stage. But it should be enough to point you in the direction of what type of information you will need to do research on, in order to write your story.

Chapter 3: Step 3 - Geography

Part of what you were doing in Chapter 2, Step 2: planning. This is specifically the geography and topography of the story. If it is set in a mansion, then what is the floorplan? How do all of the rooms connect?

If it is set in a village. What is the layout of the village. Where are the common areas?

If it is set on an aeroplane. What is the configuration of the vehicle? How many seats? Where are the galleys? Where do the crew sleep?

Everything about the geography of your story needs to be represented in diagrammatic form. Print it out and make it part of the booklet of information about your story. It is all part of the writer's guide to you, the author, actually writing your story about the information that you are gathering.

Maps, diagrams, floorplans, town plans, anything to do with the location or locations of your story is important. You have to know how every location in your story relates to every other one. You need to be absolutely clear where each stage of the story will take place.

Like a producer planning a stage play (but with way more latitude) you need to ascertain all of the stages upon which your story will be told.

Chapter 4: Step 4 - Timeline

Adding a calendar to your growing story planning guide booklet is essential. All of the main events in your story need to be set out in the order in which they happen. You will notice from my books, that I like to give my chapter titles the day and date and even the time of day in which it is set. It saves me from being too verbose in the actual chapter itself, describing the time of day and when the scene is happening.

When you are in the thick of writing you will refer to the chronology of your story often. You will be able to see when the main events are approaching. When it starts and when it concludes.

You do not necessarily have to have it in A4 size in your writer's guide booklet either. For Jack the Ripper: The Murder of Madam Athalia, I had it pasted on my wall in a dimension approximating A1 size. Think, of A3 sized paper but bigger. I would look up at it as I was writing about the many victims that Jack the Ripper murdered at his peak. I could clearly see when the next police discovery of a body was, versus when the next actual murder would take place.

You as the author need to be absolutely clear on all aspects of the chronology of your story. If you are not, it will show in your writing. The reader needs to feel that the story is progressing within the constraints of a believable frame of time.

Chapter 5: Step 5 – Detailed Plot Synopsis

Time to put some flesh on that summary that you have written. By now you should have 90% of your research done. You'll know the architecture, or the couture or the mannerisms of the period in which your book is set. You know the locations involved. And you should know the major plot points and when they happen in relation to each other.

Draw-out your summary and write a very detailed plot synopsis. You can be as detailed with the intricate parts of your story as you like. For other parts. Like bridges, that is components of the story that get you from one part to the other, you don't need to be as detailed. But overall whatever twists and turns that are the core of your story must be nutted out here. By the time you finish your detailed plot synopsis, there should be no questions that you need answered about how to resolve this plot point or that sub-plot. Everything about the story needs to be know by you at this step.

If there is any more research to be done, then now is the time. But as I have stated before, don't let it become burdensome. There has to be an end to it so that you can begin writing. Don't fuss over components that are just not important or intrinsic to the storyline.

Something that you will get better at with time, is knowing how much to research something. If for example, you are relaying a past military battle, then detail is the key, especially if you are recounting that battle as part of your story. However, if you only need to refer to it, then guess what? You don't need to spend too much time researching all of the ins and outs of it at all.

Don't become a professional student, and never leave the safe confines of study. You story awaits, and you only have one more step after this before you begin writing it.

Chapter 6: Step 6 – List of Characters

You will have done most of this already (especially for the main characters) when you were writing your detailed plot synopsis. But now is the time to get a comprehensive list together of all of the characters that will appear in your book. Don't think that you know your characters so intimately that you won't forget a first or surname during the heat of writing. It happens to the best of us.

You absolutely need a full list of the characters. The list should include physical descriptions; character and personality traits. Mannerisms of speech, accents, clothing; everything that you need in order to paint a realistic portrait of your characters. In this case however, your paint brushes are your words. The canvas, the blank pages upon which you are writing.

Keep it close. Make it a part of the booklet that you are getting together. You'll be surprised how often you will need to refer to it. Also, it may not necessarily be a finalised list. You may have to introduce a character that does something or says something that you suddenly need when you are in the thick of writing. I call these single use characters (maybe double use characters, if necessary). So ultimately, your list is flexible. Feel free to add to it as you go along.

Chapter 7: Writing the Book

Whether you are a touch-typist, or a speech to text software user, or if you prefer to write you book in long-hand on a notepad, now is the time to start writing.

You have all of the components that you need. Only the most basic formatting is required. Don't worry about page size or numbering or anything like that. There will be a time to format your book as an eBook for Google, Apple etc and there is a more constrained set of formatting rules that you will need to apply to get your book onto the Amazon print on demand system. But all of that come later! For now, you have a minimum of 500 words to write each and every sitting of your book-writing week.

Pick up that detailed plot synopsis and read the first part of your story. Expand that into the first page of your story. Just like a director directing a play, you have to take that plot, and make the characters enact it for you. Each scene that you write should have an introduction, the body of the scene that is enacted by your characters or situations and then the conclusion of that scene. A beginning, middle and end.

The overall plot is made up of many of these scenes of your characters interacting with each other; or finding themselves in a situation that they are reacting to or need in some way to deal with.

Here is where you will find what kind of writer you are. There are those that will need to describe every little bit of the scene that they are writing about. The opposite end of that spectrum is the writer that leaves a lot to the imagination of their readers and only gives the broad-brush strokes of the story.

There are sometimes that it will just roll out of you like an open tap. And other times when it will be like squeezing blood from a stone. And everything in-between. But here is where the discipline of writing is going to be instilled within you. This is a very important part of learning to be an author. I cannot overstate this enough. Do it even when you don't feel like it. Do it because it is the only way to get things done. Do it in the allotted time that you have made a sacrifice of something else in which to allocate to your writing. Do it even when you have a bad day at work and a laborious commute home.

Don't think of it as a labour or an imposition on your time, because this piece of work has a pay-back for you. The absolute satisfaction of becoming a completed manuscript that you can publish into an eBook and paperback. At then end of it you will have something to show for it.

Your detailed plot synopsis and all of the other components of your writing guide booklet are your best friend here.. Refer to them as often as needed.

What I like to do nowadays (you can see the progression of how this came about in my Author`s Notes further along in this book) is to cross off the parts of the plot that I have written. Like checking-off a list that something has been done. Component by component, you will progress through the story. Now writing it as a long-form story.

The progression from overall summary, to detailed synopsis to full-bodied work is designed to get you to write your story three times. The first two are really practice runs. Incredibly useful for getting your mind to mull over the big picture firstly, then the more detailed one, finishing off with the fully specified story that you now need to write.

Put aside all of the negative thoughts that may scuttle your desire to complete this task. Now is the time for your story to come out of you and get down on a page, electronic or otherwise.

***

There is a little trick that I introduced to my writing to ensure that I got through my allocated 500 words per sitting. And that is by not sitting. I stood up to write. If you are able, then I would encourage you to do it too. I would not allow myself to sit down until I had the entire 500-word count done in my allotted writing time.

It was then, and is now, very effective at getting me to focus on the task at hand. And that task is to write. Not sit in a comfortable chair staring out the window. You are there to write and write is what I want you to do. Don't think about writing. Just do it.

Picture the story in your head and put those visions into words and down onto the page. You will never be able to capture every last bit of the images that you see in your mind's eye. But that is not the point. The point of writing is to give the reader the opportunity to see your story. They will envision it very differently to you, even if you are very prescriptive with your writing style.

Chapter 8: Paragraphs and Chapters

Don't make your paragraphs overly long. Do not make your chapters too long. Chapters should be self-contained mini stories in their own right. It takes a bit of practice makes perfect in this instance. But don't get too caught up in this part of it whilst you are writing. I am just happy that you are now actually writing. The paragraphs and chapters can always be formatted at a later stage.

Because you are now writing your first book, and you are proving to yourself that you actually can do it, I don't want you to suffer the small stuff.

I am the master of the overly long sentence. I have actually used that failing in a later novel to deliberate intent. Read my notes further along in this book on Jack the Ripper: The Murder of Madam Athalia.

However, the longer the sentence, the more chance that your reader will get lost along the way. They may not be concentrating on reading it as much as you are on writing it. Therefore, you have to make allowances and be concise. Be obvious with your sentences. There is no need to be overly floral with you prose, unless it is called for in the setting in which your story takes place. All the best sellers of the last decade were not written by professors of literature. They were written by pragmatic Authors that want to tell a good story.

You don't have to write to an audience of Shakespearian theologians. Write to the kind of people that you think would enjoy your story. The phrasing and wording does not have to be clever. It simply has to be clear.

Chapter 9: The First Edit

The first edit is done by you. There is a secret to it that when you know it AND practice it, will reveal all sorts of problems with your sentences and paragraphs that whatever word processing software you are using, will not.

Go into a room with a printed copy of your manuscript and read it aloud. Yes, aloud. Don’t mumble. Read it as though you are reading it out to an audience.

Why?

Because you can read your work ten times in your head and it sounds perfect. But the moment it is read aloud, as if it is conversation, the problems show themselves. All of a sudden, that sentence that you read and re-read and even reworked a couple of times, seems clunky and inappropriate. If it cannot pass the reading aloud self-edit, then it needs to be changed until it sounds like it is working. And by working, I mean that as you read it, the story unfolds in your imagination. You don’t trip over sentences or ideas.

This is a remarkable way of highlighting your own errors. You can get rid of them before handing it over to a professional editor. Similarly, don’t ignore your word processing software underlining words as incorrectly spelt, or underlining sentences as it suggests a grammatic reworking.

I use Microsoft Word and it is telling me now that one part of a sentence above is basically verbose and could be made more concise. But the way that I write, is the way that I talk.

Let me share a secret with you. The first iteration of this book was a procedures manual. It was a very precise instruction book on how to write books. But I felt that it was soulless and dreary. And writing is such an emotional thing. You will connect with the words and scenes that you write about. The characters do exactly what you want them to do. They say exactly what you want them to say.

I abandoned the manual and re-wrote it in this conversational style. It is more affable and definitely more expressive about how I feel about writing. And how I want you to feel about it too.

***

The second edit; most definitely have a professional do it. Go to any of the hire-over-the-internet sites that have people that you can award the commission to. I have in the past used Guru.com and Freelancer.com but there are plenty of others.

Remember the two golden rules of hiring an editor

1. Get an editor that is sympathetic to the genre that you are writing. They need to look at it through the eyes of a reader in that genre.

2. If the alterations, criticisms or changes to the story are not designed to make your book better, get rid of that editor and find another one.

Chapter 10: ISBN

The International Sales Book Number, the ISBN is a unique identifier for your book, per book-type. Meaning, that if, like me, you self-publish through a company like Amazon as a paperback and an eBook. Then your book will need two ISBN's One for the paperback and one for the eBook.

I also publish through Smashwords, but that is only eBooks, so they get the same ISBN as the Amazon eBook. Similarly, Google Play eBooks get the same ISBN as I used for the eBook in Smashwords and Amazon.

Really, because I only have two book types that I publish through the various self-publishing portals, I only ever need to issue two ISBN's per title. One for each type. The detailed information is put into the ISBN agency portal when you have purchased the ISBN's. In fact. I knew that I was going to write a lot, so I purchased a block of ten initially, and have returned subsequently for another ten, and am about to return for yet another block of ten. It made good economic sense for me to buy them in blocks.

I have listed the overall governing agency website below, their homepage and the search function that will allow you to use the drop-down menu to select your country and find out who your regional ISBN issuer is. Here in Australia, it is Bowker-Thorpe. In Italy it is EDISER, in the U.S.A it is R.R.Bowker.

Regardless of who is the ISBN issuer in your country, find them, sign-up for an online account with them and purchase as many ISBN's as you need to get your book out there into the world, and easily identifiable.

Don't let any of the book-publishing platforms allocate one for you. Why? Because this is your work, and you can always claim absolute ownership not by just copyright, but also by pointing to the ISBN and saying, "Look it up; the online cataloguing information for that book is linked to my ISBN which I purchased from the issuing agency."

It gives me that little extra feeling of security about everything that I have ever published.

Don't be too concerned if one or more of the self-publishing platforms assign another type of unique identifier to the book. It will be their own proprietary numbering system. All of them however, will ask you if you already have an ISBN for your book. Be ready with it (or them) when it comes time to publish.

***

Note, that when you come to enter the ISBN information into the portal, you may not be able to complete it all. There are the dimensions of your book to be considered. You may not have thought of that yet. You will need to go through the Amazon Kindle Direct Publishing portal from beginning to end to make those decisions.

Don't worry, you can save the information that you have entered thus far and come back and complete it later. I'll give you a reminder in a later chapter.

https://www.isbn-international.org/

https://www.isbn-international.org/agencies

Chapter 11: Graphic Designer

I really don't know what to make of graphic designers. The very first cover for the first book that I did was as a competition on 99 designs. The idea is that you post the job and offer a set amount of money. Those graphic designers that want to make a submission do so.

Wow! I wasn't prepared for the furtive nature of some of the applicants. There were more than one that wanted to do a submission but only if the job was made private and no others could view the work but the person submitting the work and myself.

I of course, refused. I wanted to keep it in the public domain and have anyone that was on 99 designs watch the submissions come in. I got private messages from some applicants about how horrible others' submissions were. There were those that very obviously ripped-off the cover from another novel and put my title on it, thinking that any old thing would do, providing that they got paid i.e they won the competition.

If was a very eye-opening experience. Eventually however, I got it down to two or three submissions that I thought were genuinely captivating. It was those that I worked with until I got a winner.

Subsequently, I have used freelancer and guru and even one of the graphic designers that worked in the finance company that I was working for at the time of writing the murder mystery novels.

Nowadays, I have my go-to graphic designers. If I need anything I can avail myself of their talents. But the wisdom that I want to impart to you is to not be too directive about what the cover is like. You are a writer, not a designer. Allow the people that do graphic design for a living to shine through and come up with ideas for your cover that you may never have thought of.

Eventually something will really speak to you and you will have your cover. Remember that you need two types. The eBook front and back cover, as separate images. Google use both for their eBooks. And, if you choose the Amazon print-on-demand publishing, then you'll need a pdf version of the front and back covers together with the spine of the book. The thickness is dictated by the final number of pages of the book. Don't worry, the Amazon portal will tell you if you get it wrong and give you the exact dimensions required. Any graphic designer worth their salt will be able to provide the covers as desired by the various publishing platforms.

***

Speaking of covers, you will need to do the back-cover blurb. This is the marketing tool for your book. Make it exciting. Make it brief. You want it to sell the book to your reader. They must want to read it when they have read the back-cover amble.

Do me a favour and write three separate blurbs and then try them out on your friends and family. Bizarrely, you will not get a consensus on this. One will appeal to some, another to the others. It is just an exercise in getting you to realise that everyone is different. There is no hard and fast formula for making the back-cover amble excellent. All you can do is your best. Write with your heart. Ultimately, I want you to make the decision on which one has the most passion in its words.

Make sure that your graphic designer leaves room for the bar-code version of your ISBN in the bottom right-hand side of the back-cover.

Chapter 12: Amazon / Smashwords / Google / D2D

Amazon:

I love Amazon. I cannot contemplate a world without them. In fact, I don't know how I managed before they came along. This clever company more than any other has been the guiding light that others have followed when it comes to the self-publishing of books. No more are the readers of the world constrained by the publishing companies that pick and choose what is published into the book biosphere. These days, anyone can write a story and publish it for others all around the world to enjoy.

Amazon have taken it up a notch with their print-on-demand publishing. So, you can publish your book as an eBook with them, but also publish it as a paperback too. Heavenly.

Sign up with Kindle Direct Publishing and get yourself an account. It has without-doubt the easiest eBook publishing system that I have come across. The KDP portal will encourage you to publish as a paperback as well. There are a number of choices to make. The book size, the cover finish and so forth. The interface is intuitive; the instruction clear. The speed at which it pulls together novels like mine isn't going to win any awards, but I don't care. In the end I get to hold my books in my hand and feel the joy that is reading one's own work. It is a surreal experience. One that you too can indulge in.

Smashwords:

Smashwords are a fascinating company. You can publish your book as an eBook with them, and they will aggregate it to a number of other retailers on your behalf. I have chosen to do this because it is so incredibly convenient. I publish directly with Smashwords. They will sell the eBook through their website, but also push it out to:

- Apple
- Baker Taylor
- Barnes & Nobel
- Cloud Library
- Gardners
- Inktera
- Kobo
- Odilo
- Overdrive
- Scribd
- Tolino

Its absolute ease is what I love the most about publishing through Smashwords. So, get yourself an account with them and get publishing. Yes, they will charge yo a commission for this service. But (personal opinion only), it is worth it for the ease of access to the delivery channels listed above.

Note: They will push your work out to Amazon as well. But I prefer to go directly to Amazon and I'd rather not have an intermediary when it comes to them.

Google:

Oh, my dear old Google. You vex me like no other company. My day job is as a Business Analyst for a media company (I've only just started with them). Previously I worked for a financial software company, prior to that a mortgage wholesaler, and prior to that a facilities management company. My point is, that I am not stupid. And yet I have major problems publishing with Google. It has the hardest to use eBook publishing platform that I have come across. Which seems to be contrary to their usual way of leading the way when it comes to innovation. Take Google maps for example, and Google Street View. I couldn't imagine a world without them. But as for the Google Play Book Publishing. I have to admit having gone running to Guru.com in order to find someone that can do it for me.

When thwarted by the insurmountable, find an expert that can do it for you.

Note: It is the Google Play version of your eBook that requires the file uploaded to the Partner Portal to have both a front cover as the header image and the back cover as the suffix image.

Draft 2 Digital:

I must confess that I had never heard of this aggregator before last month. They appear to have the same a similar partner list as Smashwords. However, the entire process looks to be even easier. I have yet to publish anything with Draft to Digital yet. Perhaps I will, just to check off the sales channels that Smashwords have not. The current distribution channel list is:

- Amazon
- Apple
- Barnes & Nobel
- Kobo
- Scribd
- Playster
- Overdrive
- Tolino
- 24Symbols

I suppose from my point of view it would be nice to have access to Playster and 24Symbols. I can't help but think that the future holds some rationalisation in the eBook distribution channel arena. Exactly who will survive and who will not is very unclear to say the least. Maybe they all will. But if not, best to mitigate that risk and publish through as many distribution channels as possible.

Xinxii:

Pronounced zin-zee, this is an unusual book publishing platform. They say that they are Europe's largest independent eBook publishing platform. The one thing that I really like about Xinxii is that you can choose to receive you royalties from sales in one of three currencies. I have chosen the Great British Pound, simply because it always seems to be stronger than the Australian Dollar. When the commission is converted from GBP to AUD, it ends up in my favour. I also have the choice of Euro or US Dollars. For now, I'll stick with GBP.

Here is the list of distribution channels that they partner with:

- Amazon
- Apple
- Angus & Robertson
- Buch.de
- Buecher.de
- Casa del Libro
- Family Christian Stores
- Fnac
- Google Play
- Hugendubel
- Indigo
- Kobo
- Libris
- Livraria Cultura
- Mondadori

- Nook
- Rakuten
- Scribd
- Thalia
- Weltbild
- Whitcoulls
- WH Smith

Simply because of their reach, they are worth putting up with a user interface that looks like it comes from the mid 1990's

***

Tax Number:

I have my own company registered here in Australia. Aenghus Chisholme is listed as a sole-trader. Nothing fancy. But, simply to allow the Australian Government to see that I am writing and self-publishing books around the world, it is useful. However, all of my publishers are domiciled overseas. Which presents a taxation question; where do I pay tax for my sales? Lucky for me Australia and the United States have a reciprocal taxation agreement. Meaning, that I was allowed to apply for a foreign-national US tax number. The process is arduous. But I have been able to register my Kindle Direct and Smashwords accounts with that tax number so that Amazon and Smashwords (and probably Google, I'll have to go back into my account and check it), will not take tax from me. I am expected to pay my tax to the

Australian Taxation Office instead. Which seems fair, after all, I do live here and not there. Go to the Internal Revenue Service website (in the US) and search for "Individual Taxpayer Identification Number"

Chapter 13: Set Up a Google Alert

You will want to know when people write about your book. So, best to give it a title that is rather unique. That way, when you set up a Google alert, the results that you receive are more than likely going to be about your book, rather than happenstance that an article somewhere had mentioned the title.

This is as simple as getting a gmail account, meaning a Google account of some description and then do a Google search on setting up an alert. Easy.

Chapter 14: Lodge with Federal and State Libraries

This is a requirement that you may not be aware of. You will need to do research on the rules applicable in your particular country, however it holds true for most of the world. If you publish a book, it will need to be printed at your expense, and lodged with your federal and state library. Or, if you don't have states, like New Zealand, then just the National Library.

They are entrusted with keeping a copy of every book ever published by native authors. This is of course only applicable to paperbacks, and hardcovers, not audio books and eBooks. Although, you can bet that that situation will change sometime in the future.

I have a backlog of publications to send to the National Library of Australia and the Library of New South Wales. But, that is owing to a rather grey area. Allow me to explain.

My first book was self-published. I may have had it printed overseas, but it was delivered to Port Sydney ready for distribution. Therefore, it was subject to this rule. I had to send a copy to our nation's capital Canberra, and one to the State Library here in Sydney.

I included the cataloguing-in-publication entry notes in-lieu of the normal copyright information that you see now at the front of all of my books. It read like this:

National Library of Australia Cataloguing-in-Publication entry

Author: Chishome, Aenghus

Title: AD 491 :Merlin the Sorcerer / Aenghus Chisholme

ISBN: 9780987272003 (pbk)

Subjects: Merlin (Legendary character) – fiction

Historical Fiction,

Dewey Number: A823.4

Can you see the problem to which I am referring?

Every successive book that has been published as been with the print-on-demand system available via Amazon. And I publish through the KDP portal which is part of the US site. So ultimately it is printed overseas and then brought into the country on a sale-by-sale basis. I began to think that it wasn't the same as printing in a batch and then importing them for either sale or distribution as marketing material.

However, the onus is on me, as the publisher domiciled here in Australia to provide these copies to the Federal and State libraries. Ultimately, I have decided to do the right thing and provide these copies at my expense to the relevant parties. And so should you. This book is all about not procrastinating anymore. Best that I expand that to include the administrative components of writing and self-publishing.

Chapter 15: Repeat

If you have only ever wanted to write one story and this book has helped you to do that then I congratulate you. The sense of accomplishment is no-doubt invigorating. But, if you have reached this point and have decided that you have another story to write, then it's time to go back to the planning phase and get it done.

By all means give yourself a small break to revel in your achievement. You'll need some time to do marketing either via regular channels like advertising in book publications or social media channels, twitter, Facebook, Instagram and all of the others. However, marketing is not something that I go into in any depth for a good reason. I tend to leave that to the experts. Do a Google search on how to market your self-published book and watch what comes back in the results list.

Stick with the most popular. The ones that can prove that their methods work. And those that have satisfied customer reviews, that don't look suspicious or fraudulent. You don't want to spend a fortune on marketing and get no sales. That would be as demotivating as a vitriolic editor critiquing your work.

I suppose the one lesson that I can give you with absolute assuredness is that there is no single solution that can absolutely guarantee results. If there was, everybody would be using it, and it would not be a secret. You certainly wouldn't have to go looking for it, if it did exist.

On the other hand, book sales may not be the goal for you. The accomplishment alone could be the satisfaction that you derive. Let's face it, there are a lot of people out there that think that they have a novel inside of them. And that they are going to sit down and write it one day. But if that were to come true, then the human bibliotheca of literature would be twice as big as it is today. Procrastination for a lifetime is a human characteristic that we are all capable of wallowing in.

Don't be one of them; be a writer!

Chapter 16: Repeat; Again

And so, it goes on. If you make it through your second book writing experience. Then you are sure to do a third, and fourth etcetera. This is my ninth book and I am showing no signs of slowing down.

Something that I started in 2010 as an exercise to see if I could actually do it, has become a very important part of my leisure time. I wouldn't be without it. Sure, there are times when I take a break from it. But restlessness soon begins to pervade, and it becomes difficult for me to stay away from writing.

I want the writing bug to take hold of you too. If you can get that one story out of your head and into words, then you may find that another story starts to make itself known. Therefore, another book must be written.

It is true of me, that when I finish a story, I consider it done. Although the immediacy of eBook and print-on-demand publishing means that I can go back and make changes, I rarely do. In fact, quite the opposite. Once that story is written, it is out of my head and the next is filling up my thoughts. If you were to ask me about some of the finer detail in any of my completed books, then I would struggle to give you a comprehensive answer without re-reading it for myself. I believe that the book is written, therefore the story is told, and I no longer need to think about it anymore.

It is a fantastic feeling. I don't feel that I have abandoned the story that I created. I feel that I have released it; given life to it for anyone who reads and enjoys it. I hope that you feel the same way too. Write to me at author@aenghuschisholme.com and let me know what feelings you encounter at the nexus of your writing journey. I imagine that there will be as many similarities as there will be differences with all of you that follow the guidelines and turn a dream into a written-reality.

Chapter 17: Author's Notes

I think that it would be beneficial to put on display for you the ups and downs of the books that I have written thus far. Below you will find the summaries of the novels and otherwise that I have authored to date.

This book is really a personal plea for you, who are reading, to become a writer too. It can be done; and you can do it. There is no need to think about it endlessly. The story won't become better and better over the years like a fine wine. It will become mouldy and stagnant. You, for the sake of your own self, need to get it out of your head and into book form. Then you can think clearly about what else you want to do.

I hope that you will be thinking about writing a second book. But, even if you aren't, then you will be contemplating something entirely new. Something other than wondering what it would be like to write that story once and for all. Release yourself. Open up new possibilities. Explore a new trail. Give yourself the freedom to move beyond that thought of 'one day I will write this story'. Because when you do, nobody knows what will happen.

All of this time, you may have been blocking another entirely new thought, with the 'one day I'll write' one. Writing can be a cathartic. I certainly find that it is. And so, I do it over and over again; because I want to and have an inner desire and need to.

What is it that you should be doing instead of wondering?

Merlin the Sorcerer AD491

Paperback ISBN 978-0-6480789-0-6
eBook ISBN 978-0-9872720-1-0

Back cover amble:

Merlin embarks on a passionate affair with Morgan Le Fay, sister to King Arthur. But the beautiful and other-worldly Fairy Nimue has other ideas for Merlin.

King Arthur is facing battle with the murderous Saxon overlord Aelle. Meanwhile the self-absorbed ruler of the Fairy people, Hellekin, is set to intervene in Arthur's battle because of Nimue's involvement with the humans. This causes a situation that may tip the balance of power to the invading warmonger.

Enter a tangled web if intrigue and lust, sorcery and sword fights, as the lives of these mythical figures intersect and irrevocably change the natural course of events in the year 491AD.

Author's Notes:

Approximately = 94,000 words.

Writing Time = 11 months. Including, editing and re-writes. 500 words per sitting. Or rather, standing.

i. Editor:

Editing was done via Freelancer.com. I don't recall the name of the lady, but she did a good job. I did the first edit as I have stated that you should, in this self-help book. But the second edit was done by a professional. Let me tell you a little about editors. If they are over-critical and not helping you make a better product, then get rid of them.

You do not need somebody shooting you down in flames, especially for your first book. Do not take criticism of the storyline or plot line unless it is specifically pointing out a hole in the storyline. You need to choose an editor that is sympathetic with your genre. For my second and I think, third books in this series I hired a fellow fantasy author by the name of Greg Strandberg. He was absolutely fantastic. I encourage you to do the same. Let me tell you a little story. I knew someone that had been an editor of a local newspaper for a while. I gave her a pre-release printed manuscript copy of Merlin the Sorcerer. After much cajoling she finally came back to me with a three-page diatribe of exactly how terrible the first page of my book was.

She shot holes in everything and managed to criticise it taking more words than appears in on the first page of my book. In fact, about three times as many words. Not helpful. In the end I ignored all of it. She was just not a fan of sword-and-sorcery stories. She couldn't bring herself to suspend disbelief as you need to do as a reader and editor in this category.

If you are writing crime, then find an editor that has done lots of editing in that genre. Whatever the field of your story, you need an editor that knows that genus and will respond appropriately with constructive criticism. An editor should help you make your work better. Not drive you away from writing altogether.

ii. Plot Synopsis:

I was ineffably snobbish with the original iteration of this book. There are about 500 printed copies (with an entirely different cover to the one that you see on Amazon today). The chapter titles were Latin statements of the Julian Calendar, alongside their Druitt calendar counterparts. I have subsequently divested the book of those chapter headings, and they are now in English.

iii. Formatting the paperback:

Typesetting was one in India, via Freelancer.com. Printing was done in China. And I managed to get all 500 copies printed, shipped and delivered to Port Botany here in Sydney for $1.93 CIF per book. That is Cost, Insurance & Freight. Let me be more specific. Printing costs as well as packing them up in boxes and shipping them from China to Sydney and all covered with shipping insurance. All for $1.93

Australian Dollars per copy. Multiply that by 500 and you get a very reasonable cost for my first outing as a self-published author. Of course, nowadays we have the miracle of Amazon, print-on-demand. So, there is no need to do things like that.

In case you ever come across one of those very limited edition of 500 first printed copies the ISBN is 978-0-9872720-0-3

iv. Characters:

The characters that you expect are all there, except for any additives that Sir Thomas Mallory gave to the Arthurian legend in his tome Le Mort De Arthur (The Death of Arthur). Therefore, there is no Camelot, no Lancelot, and no quest for the holy grail.

In the fifth century, the knights would not have been Christian. As Christianity was only beginning to take hold in the British Isles back then.

Kings did not build a castle and live in it, ruling over their land. They were nomadic and would have had a number of castles which they travelled around to throughout the year. I made use of this in subsequent books.

In my telling of this story, the original Welsh tomes gave me characters that I could do more interesting things with. Morgan Le Fay for example, half-sister to Arthur. If she was a woman alone in the fifth century and Arthur offered her sanctuary in his court, then you can bet that she would not be busy planning his demise. It was great fun to write about familiar characters acting in unfamiliar and unexpected ways.

v. The writing process:

My detailed notes were printed out. I cut them up with scissors into paragraphs and then stuck those paragraphs on a large calendar of the year 491AD that I had printed out. This gave the story its flow. It was visually represented to me every time I looked up at the wall. Then, to write the story, I would pick off a paragraph and expand it.

Some paragraphs were expanded into full pages, others even more. I followed the rules that I set out in the chapter 'Writing the Book' here. Each plot point was written with a way to introduce the scene. I would describe the scene and how the characters acted-out their roles within it, and then the scene would have an exit, or conclusion or bridge to the next scene.

Paragraph by paragraph, I picked off the storyline from the calendar but by bit. Then one day, it was done. Success. My point had been proven. I could write a cohesive novel. If I can do it, then you can do it too.

vi. Mistakes:

I set the story over the course of one year. January to December. The chapters were named after each month. They included all that I had planned to happen in the story for that month. And I found that the majority of it took part in October. The chapter became so long that I eventually had to break it into three separate parts. Mistake to avoid? Do not make your chapters overly long. As a reader, think of how you react to chapters that seem to go on and on.

Guinevere the Queen AD494

Paperback ISBN 978-0-6480789-1-3
eBook ISBN 978-0-9872720-2-7

Back cover amble:
The magical sword Excalibur, the very symbol of King Arthur`s power, has been stolen. Unable to defer mediation in a conflict over Hadrian's Wall in the north of his monarchy, Arthur and Merlin are unable to immediately search for the thief.

Queen Guinevere and Sorceress Morgan Le Fay set out unbeknown to Arthur to find the sword. Accompanied by the three brother-Knights Sir Galahad, Sir Gareth and Sir Gawain, they traverse Saxon-held lands in search of the thief.

The Queen and Sorceress will have to bargain with magical creatures and battle with a mythological beast in order to recover the sword. To do this they travel to Roman-occupied Gaul. Danger awaits them at ever turn in a far away land in the year AD494.

Author's Notes:

Approximately = 84,000 words.

Writing Time = 6 months. Including, editing and re-writes. 1000 words per sitting. Or rather, standing.

i. Editor:

Editing was done via Freelancer.com by the before mentioned Greg Strandberg. Excellent job he did too. That is the second edit. I, of course, did the first edit.

ii. Chapters:

Notice how this book is about ten-thousand words less than the first, but it has many more chapters. I had pretty much figured out that the overly long chapters on the first novel were doing my story a dis-service. This one has 52 Chapters, which is more befitting a story of approximately 84,000 words.

iii. Plot Synopsis:

The first book was very Machiavellian. It was all about mystery and intrigue and people deceiving people by pretending to be something other than who they are. I thought that it was very appropriate for an Arthurian court novel. However, for this book I wanted to shake things up a little. So, this was much more action/adventure; almost swashbuckling. I'm glad that I did it too. It was a stretch for me to keep two parallel stories going, the Arthur Merlin story in the north and the Guinevere and Morgan story in

Gaul. I wanted the female characters to have the lead in this story and behave as strong Celtic-blooded warriors.

Just as I had finished-off the first book with a little teaser as to what the second would hold. I did the same here. The epilogue is a pointer to how vengeful the ruler of the fairy people felt. He would be sure to return for his revenge. And if course he did.

iv. Characters:

The original Welsh spelling for some of the character names was not doing me any favours with sales. So, I altered them back to the more accepted modern-day spellings. At least in the title of the book, the book cover and the back-cover amble. I similarly altered the ISBN registration entry to reflect this. Thus Gwenhwyvar (gwen-hth-var) became Guinevere. Sir Guaen (goo-way-en) became Gawain. There was a point where I was writing a bridge. That is a part of the story that was not intrinsic to the outcome of the plot. The characters were travelling from one place to another and had camped out. There was a intervention by some of the bad-guys and then Fairy intervention. I read it back and though that it was a bit lifeless, so I interjected a little bloodied swordsmanship into the scene.

It worked quite a treat too. When I was reading (aloud) the book to myself as part of the first edit, I came to the scene. I had totally forgotten about the interjected sub-plot-point, as it wasn't on the summary or the detailed plot synopsis. And when I read it I recall recoiling and shouting out "she killed them!?" I couldn't believe my eyes. Someone had re-written part of my book; but how? It took a few moments for my memory to return and realise that I had in fact done it. But for those brief moments I was convinced that I was reading somebody's else's work.

v. The writing process:

I stuck rigidly to my minimum word count of 1000 words per writing session. Sometimes I would go way over, but that is fine. If the mood takes you, please just continue to write. But never, ever do yourself a discredit and fail to make your minimum word count.

It didn't feel like an imposition moving up from 500 words to 1000. In fact, the whole process seemed easier the second time around. I think this was helped by the fact that it was written twice as fast. 1000 words can be quite a good scene. I noticed that it was easier to write a scene in 1000 words than it was in 500 words.

The transition to writing more words each session, actually helped me trim my writing style from the first to the second book. That is reflected in the number of overall words of the second book, but it has a more complex storyline. Less words; more story. I would take that learning from one book to the next from this point onwards.

The first book set the scene but progressing the same characters into another story was easier for me as the author, because I didn't have to explain as much about who they were, what they were like and where they came from. Having said that you will probably be surprised by the next paragraph. But it is good advice, so please learn from my mistakes and don't make them yourself.

vi. Mistakes:

I shouldn't have written a series. Eagle eyed fans will know that the Arthurian series was originally meant to be six books. But I truncated it down to four books so that I could try my hand and a completely different genre.

Writing books is like writing songs; you keep writing till you get a hit. Then people will become interested in your back-catalogue.

The hardest and best thing that I have ever done as an author is change genres. I encourage you to do it as often as you can. It flexes your muscles as a writer and forces you into situations that need inventiveness to get yourself out of.

Unless your first book is a sales hit, and your readers demand a sequel, then it is better to test the waters of readership with as many and varied stories that you can invent and get them out into the world. Something will resonate and signal you that you are on the right track. You don't want to commit to writing an America civil-war epic series of tomes if there just isn't the interest in it that you think that there is.

Don't be offended. Be versatile. Ultimately my Arthurian books found their audience, but in retrospect I should have written my first murder / mystery novel a lot sooner than I did. I am haunted by the question "what if.." What if I write a romance novel and it is a global hit?

What if you write a book in a genre that you would never normally contemplate. And it resonates with a broad audience. If you never try it, you'll never know?

It's been said that by trying to please everyone, you end up pleasing no-one. However, in the case of writing books, if you try to please the maximum amount of reading audience tribes, you may hit the target of popularity in a genre that you had never expected to.

Ian Fleming became famous in the 1950's because of his James Bond novels. But did you know that he also wrote Chitty-Chitty-Bang-Bang: The Magical Car. It was well received back in 1964 when it was released. The radical departure from his Bond novels was jarring to some critics. But it was a success nevertheless.

For my future, there is a science fiction book (a one-off story) and a Spy Thriller (a one-off story) and a children's book (a one-off story) all next off the ranks from me. I have a want and a need to write something in every genre that I can think of. Maybe because I know how intoxicating it is to create a story in a category that you have never contemplated before.

It really will test your mettle as a writer. But the only way to get better at your craft is to exercise your muscles as an author and changing genres will certainly do that for you.

Sir Gawain and the Green Knight AD499

Paperback ISBN 978-0-6480789-6-8
eBook ISBN 978-0-9872720-3-4

Back cover amble:

Sir Gawain, one of Arthur`s most trusted Knights, is under attack from a supernatural being. The Green Knight is an unstoppable animated corpse, hell-bent upon Gawain`s death. The only two magical beings in Caerleon Castle that have any hope of opposing this evil are powerless whenever the Green Knight is near.

Desperate for help Merlin turns to Queen Nimue of the fairy people. In an alliance forged from need the mystical beings unravel the circumstances that cause the appearance of the Green Knight at every full-moon.

With each ensuing attack the Green Knight becomes more powerful and more cunning. Can the alliance between the fairy people and King Arthur`s court overcome their mistrust of each other in order to battle the very embodiment of evil?

Author's Notes:

Approximately = 73,000 words.

Writing Time = 3 months. Including, editing and re-writes. 2000 words per sitting. Or rather, standing.

i. Editor:

Editing (the second edit) was done via Freelancer.com by the fiction author Greg Strandberg.

ii. Chapters:

Again, I had managed to trim the number of words in my book but still put together an intricate story. I was definitely getting better with each successive novel, and it was showing. By a pure coincidence this book has 52 Chapters just as the book Guinevere did. It was not something that I particularly aimed for. It just turned out like that.

iii. Plot Synopsis:

This was my ode to Stephen King. Why? Why not? He is a prolific author that has been published for decades and has won numerous awards. I wanted this book to be a horror novel. The original Welsh tome of the Green Knight was a morality story. It was a humiliation of Sir Gawain and his immature nature. The Green Knight taught him a lesson in humility. A trait necessary for a Knight.

Mine however, was outright horror. The Green Knight in question was a resurrected corpse. I ensured that his magic was such that it prevented any help from Merlin and

Morgan. Thus, the Arthurian court is under siege from a single Knight. In this case all the King`s horses and all the King`s men, could not stop the killer corpse.

iv. Characters:

I introduced an alliance between two already known characters. What is better than one baddie? Two baddies of course.

Any other characters were basically added into the story for the sake of the plot. I was surprised at how some of them became instantly likeable. The smaller characters in this book are something that I am very proud of. It is a learning that I have taken into every successive novel. Making the non-main characters believable is important in making your entire story believable. Quite a feat when writing sword and sorcery fantasy. Nevertheless, I succeeded.

v. The writing process:

This was again, easier than the previous book. As before, I did not notice the increase from 1000 words to 2000 words per session. But as I still have a full-time job and I do all of my writing between 7:30pm and 9:30pm in the evening, Monday, Tuesday, Wednesday and Thursday, I found that I was fitting 2000 words into the 2 hours easily enough. The idea of increasing to 3000 for my next novel did occur to me. But I found that I could not easily fit 3000 words into the two hours of my evening time that I have to dedicate to it. (In case you are wondering; I go to bed at 9:30pm. Early for some, but perfect for me.)

I though whilst writing my first book that 500 words was good for a scene. Until I wrote my second and discovered that 1000 was better for writing a good scene. Imagine my surprise to find that 2000 is much better. It allows the freedom to stretch the scene into a better shape. I attribute this to the fact that this book takes a number of twists and turns but is a very seamless story. As the saying goes, practice makes perfect.

vi. Mistakes:

Surprisingly few. I recall that the first edit that I did showed up far less clunky sentences and other problems than the first two books. Perhaps the idea that you should write 2000 words in 2 hours should be applicable as an author's standard of some kind?

I originally had a small caveat at the end of this novel stating that there would be two un-written novels in the series, and I would skip ahead to the final one so that I could get into writing murder-mystery instead. I subsequently removed this from most of the books (I think that the Google Play eBook version may still have it). There is no need for your readers to know what is going on in your project planning of novels.

Arthur the King AD517

Paperback ISBN 978-0-6480789-3-7
eBook ISBN 978-0-9872720-4-1

Back Cover Amble:

King Arthur rules the largest Monarchy in the history of Britain. Frustrated that he has not yet driven all of the Saxons, Angles, and Jutes form the land he embarks on a series of savage battles within his own borders.

Prince Amhar, Arthur's only legitimate son opposes his father's tactics and reasoning. Along with his half-brother Mordrede, they offer support to the township of Camlann, the site of Arthur's next planned assault.

Magicians Morgan Le Fay and Merlin take opposing viewpoints over the King's actions and a rift is formed in their twenty-seven-year friendship.

Will Arthur wage war against his own flesh-and-blood, risking a schism within his Kingdom in order to fulfil his desire for a country purged of the invaders?

Author's Notes:

Approximately = 85,000 words.

Writing Time = 3 months. Including, editing and re-writes. 2000 words per standing.

i. Editor:

Editing (the second edit) was done via Freelancer.com by a specialist in the fantasy genre.

ii. Chapters:

You guessed it, yes, this too has 52 Chapters just as Guinevere and Gawain did. I am not particularly superstitious, but I do note that I managed through happenstance to not only make three of the four books 52 Chapters, but I also began all four of them on a full-moon. It was quite a coincidence that I would be writing away here in the spare attic-style bedroom. Eventually after completing my allotted words, I would look out at the night sky. Full moon, each and every time I began one of these novels. Given that the symbolism of the moon plays a part in each of the stories it could be my inspiration has a lunar tidal ebb and flow. Only time will tell I suppose.

iii. Plot Synopsis:

I put myself in the unenviable position of needing to come up with the back-cover blurb before I had done the detailed plot synopsis. This was because I had engaged a designer to give me four covers, all a cohesive set with similar design theme. You'll find that they are still used on the Smashwords eBooks. But for the others, I have subsequently traded covers yet again. Although this was because the paperbacks needed a very different format and dots per inch resolution. Thus, it was just easier to re-do the lot of them.

Nevertheless, I found myself wanting to alter a few things here and there when I finally did the detailed plot synopsis. But then I felt a little constrained because I did not want to deviate too far from the original back-cover amble that I had come up with. It did make for a more disciplined kind of story creation on my part.

iv. Characters:

This is really all about the youngsters in the court and their differing ideas to the entrenched generation. I introduced a young go-getter Sir Dynadane. And Mordrede and Amhar are now all grown-up and fully-fledged Knights of the Round Table. All with minds of their own. Ultimately, I had given myself the unenviable task of almost demonising King Arthur. He needed a foil for these intransigent ways and what better to do that then by highlighting the generation-gap. Old ways and new ways clashing head to head, or in this case, father to sons.

A plausible way had to be found to finish the story, and yet have his remaining followers disband the old Kingdom, in favour of a new way of life. Working that into the accepted myth that Arthur went to war with his illegitimate son

Mordrede gave me quite a challenge from the point of view of constructing a story that highlighted the evils of racism.

As with all of the Arthur series, they are filled with modern-day messages but set back in the fourth and fifth centuries.

v. The writing process:

I was very hard on myself with this one because I wanted to publish it on my birthday in that year. So, I typed like a man possessed. Often going beyond my 2000 wordcount per session.

I can tell you that the result was immensely pleasing for me. I reached my deadline and got the book published on my November birthday back in 2014. Then I gave myself all of December 2014 and January 2015 off writing to recharge my batteries.

It worked. My next novel benefitted from the down-time. I was re-energised and more enthusiastic than ever to get it done.

vi. Mistakes:

Apart from trying to write a back-cover amble before properly planning the entire story, I cannot say that I made any mistakes with this one. Practice really does make perfect.

If it didn’t get easier, and if you don’t become better with each successive book, then it would be very disheartening. Don’t misinterpret what I am saying here. There are always going to be days when you are forcing it out of you. But by now, those days are very few and far between for me. So, take heart, the more you do, the better you’ll become.

Murder on the Mary Celeste

Paperback ISBN 978-0-6480789-4-4
eBook ISBN 978-0-9872720-5-8

Back cover amble:

1871 – Somewhere on the Atlantic Ocean:

A ruthless killer is murdering the passengers and crew aboard the merchant Brigantine sailing ship Mary Celeste.

Alone on a tumultuous sea and far from help, they are all but defenceless against the unseen assassin.

Suspicion is directed at one then the other as they grapple with the reality that one of their number is perpetrating these horrible crimes.

Author's Notes:

Approximately = 87,000 words.

Writing Time = 3 months. Including, editing and re-writes. 2000 words per session.

i. Editor:

Editing was done via Freelancer.com. I was happy with the results.

ii. Plot Synopsis:

I had committed to writing a crime-thriller in the same vein as the book (and subsequent movie; "Smilla's Sense of Snow" an absolutely beautifully written and thought-out book by Peter Hoeg. Why this was a particular inspiration is that you can go through the book or watch the movie and think for 9/10th of the experience that it is a human interest and\or detective thriller. But then at the end it takes an unexpected twist and you realise that it could easily be classified as something else entirely; science-fiction perhaps?

So, within this in mind, I set about writing a book on how, alone at sea, the passengers and crew of the Mary Celeste are picked-off one-by-one. In many ways it was an homage to Agatha Christie's work too. I give the reader enough crumbs of information to figure out what is going on. But making the leap from crime-thriller to supernatural-thriller is not evident until the very end of the book.

For those that have come back to me and said that they were never expecting it to have an ending like that, I say; read it again, and then you'll recognise all of the pointers that I put throughout the story that should have alerted you.

iii. Characters:

I took a degree of licence with the characters. The actual Mary Celeste passengers and crew may very well have living relatives that could object to their ancestors being the subject of a work of fiction. So, I set the book a couple of years out from the real Mary Celeste mystery. And altered the names of the people involved just enough to imbue them with my ownership.

There were just enough of them on the ship for me to deal with in an ensemble way. Each of the characters gets his or her own back-story. Some have very duplicitous lives indeed, as we discover along the way. The entire story plays like a mini-series or a movie. It was not meant to come out that way, it just seemed to happen. Ultimately, this is where I have excelled with character development. For that learning alone, it was worth me writing this book. To this day, it remains my favourite

iv. The writing process:

I had everything plastered over the walls of my spare room. A detailed deck plan of the Mary Celeste. I had the actual course that it sailed mapped on a colour chart. I knew the dates that it departed New York Harbour and when it arrived at the Azores. And when it was found adrift, abandoned for no apparent reason.

In short, I followed my own normal practice for this one, and the writing process couldn't have been easier.

v. Mistakes:

The only mistake in this instance was one of assumption. I had assumed that the Mary Celeste was a large sailing ship. It was not. It was small. This left me in a position of difficulty. How was I going to start bumping-off the passengers and crew without anyone noticing, at least initially? It was quite a conundrum. But I rose to the challenge and in the end, it turned out to be a strength. I had to become very inventive with the ways that people died. For the first couple, it had to look like unfortunate accidents. It isn't until later that the magnitude of the problem is revealed to the rest. They are harbouring a murderer, and he or she wants to kill each and every one of them.

Jack the Ripper: The murder of Madam Athalia

Paperback ISBN 978-0-6480789-5-1
eBook ISBN 978-0-9872720-6-5

Back cover amble:
London 1888: The most horrific murders are being committed in Whitechapel one after the other. The police have no clues. The killer eludes them every time. Nobody connects the death of an old psychic in a grand manor house far from the slums of the inner-city with the spate of murders. But one clever junior detective sees a bizarre similarity. If he can solve the clues it will lead him to unmask, Jack the Ripper.

Author's Notes:

Approximately = 79,000 words.

Writing Time = 3 months. Including, editing and re-writes. 2000 words per session

i. Editor:

Editing was done via Freelancer.com.

ii. Chapters:

49 chapters, and a new experiment for me. I began to think that readers in this day-and-age are pressed for time. Most people that I see reading are usually commuting to and from work. Therefore, I decided to try and alter my writing style to suit. Meaning, that the overall sentences are longer. The paragraphs, comparatively shorter. The idea being to get as much story pushed out in as few words as possible. And it worked. The first time that I read this back to myself, I was surprised the pace of the story.

iii. Plot Synopsis:

I was in a little bit of a writing bind with this book, the second in a murder-mystery trilogy. What if someone read this book first and then went back to read the first. There should still be a surprise for the reader no matter what. So I worked it in such a way that if a reader does start with this, the second book, they can go back to book number one, they still won't really know who the real culprit is.

iv. Characters:

I gave this book a dashing and ambition young hero. Engaged to a social climbing lady of the day and each with a set of parents that gave the young couple a real good finishing touch.

The doomed Madam Athalia in the title was mentioned in Murder on the Mary Celeste. But here we see her in the winter years of her life. Happily, retired and living in the splendour that her psychic abilities have been able to afford her.

The rest of the characters are well known. There are a number of murders attributed to Jack the Ripper, but only five of which are absolutely without question. These are the ones that I focused upon in the story. They get bumped-off at a rather alarming rate.

The investigative team too are well documented, so I make mention of all of them at one stage or another.

v. The writing process:

Because I was basing my story in and around the actual deaths and the turn of events in the investigation of the murders, it felt very easy to write this book. My story is woven into the fabric of what happened. However, as we know, the supernatural being that is committing the crimes is basically untouchable because the police are looking for a manic human rather than a creature from the depths in human form. The gradual realisation by Detective Gates that all is not what it appears is what unwittingly puts himself in the firing line of Jack the Ripper.

Aided in the beginning by the psychic abilities of Alice Athalia, we see the young Detective come close to his prize but not quite. And then with the loss of Athalia (supposed loss) he has to make his own way into the world of the monster alone.

vi. Mistakes:

As a sequel to Murder on the Mary Celeste, this is a very well-constructed story, executed with a good deal of finesse. High praise for myself I know. But proof that you really do get better at writing the more that you do it.

The Monster of Matlock

Paperback ISBN 978-0-6480789-7-5
eBook ISBN 978-0-9872720-9-6

Back Cover Amble:

Derbyshire, England: Matlock and Matlock Bath are Edwardian towns clinging to the side of a steep and heavily forested gorge. The river Derwent snakes through the valley below. They are idyllic places in which to live.

But in the year 1893 something is lurking in the mists that roll down the valley. Hideous and relentless, it is murdering the inhabitants but masquerading the deaths in a fiendish way. The townspeople are divided. Are they victims of an irresistible force or is it just unfortunate happenstance?

Author's Notes:

Approximately = 68,000 words.

Writing Time = 2.5 months. Including, editing and re-writes. 2000 words per session

i. Editor:

Editing (the second edit) was done via Freelancer.com by a specialist in the murder-mystery genre.

ii. Chapters:

Only 31 Chapters, and a comparatively short book when compared to my others. Nevertheless, I was very happy with how this turned out. Proof that sometimes you don't need a lot of words to express a neat and tidy story.

iii. Plot Synopsis:

I wanted to finish off the trilogy once and for all. I saw Matlock Bath on an episode of "Escape to the Country", a British lifestyle show that helps city-folk migrate to the countryside. From the moment that I saw Matlock Bath I knew that I wanted to set a horror story there. Sure enough, my research uncovered a murder in the year 1891 of one Martha Morell who was shot through the window of her home whilst sitting in a chair reading the paper. The crime was never solved. I had to move the date out to 1893 to fit it in with my other books. And to coincide with the opening of their cable-car tram which was built in the neighbouring town of Matlock. And Mrs Morell inherited the maiden name of Athalia. She became the only sister of Madam Alice Athalia. It was perfect.

It had all of the ingredients for an atmospheric horror story. The main protagonist this time was not a detective. He just happened to be in a town where people start to get killed. Or rather, dying in unusual ways. The deaths could be taken for misadventure. But he begins to think that there is something else at work.

Having Alice Athalia's married sister living in the town, it naturally has a séance or two and communion with the spirits from the great beyond. The occasional sighting of a monster in the misty landscape was the finishing touch. More than any other of my books the overall and then detailed plot synopsis came together very easily. Up to a point. See below 'the writing process' for what ended up happening.

iv. Characters:

Matlock and Matlock Bath had quite a history in the field of hydropathic establishments in the victorian age. And the people that built and ran them are part of that history. I was able to incorporate a number of them into the book.

The main protagonist is a complete fabrication. He happens to have the same surname of the establishment that he is managing. It just made it easier to always associate him with the Smedly Hydro business. A good man in a bad situation; perfect.

The gregarious mayor too is an amalgamation of character traits that I have seen in mayors here in Sydney and throughout many an old western movie enjoyed in my youth.

There are a lot of cameo appearances of previous characters thanks to the psychic abilities of Martha Morell and because the dead tend not to rest if they have been brutally murdered. There is always recourse, even from beyond the grave.

v. The writing process:

Everything seemed to be going very well indeed and then at the very end of the book I was left entirely flat. I did not like the ending at all. So, I did something that I have not done before, I changed it completely. By consulting Google maps and re-familiarising, myself in even further detail of the topography of Matlock and Matlock Bath, I invented an entirely new ending that really satisfied me.

This was a good learning experience for me. I never normally deviate from my detailed plot synopsis. But in this instance, I simply could not stop myself. Ultimately, I did not want the ending to be a mediocre one. Looking back, I'm very glad that I changed it significantly. The whole thing now reads as a very entertaining story wrapped around a real event at the end of the 19th Century in Matlock and Matlock Bath.

vi. Mistakes:

It was hard to make a mistake with this one as the history of both towns is so well documented in pictures and words. I even found an original parish map of the area from the period. I had it blown up to A1 size so that I could see it properly and reference where everything was at the time.

The circumstances surrounding the murder of Martha Morell are also well documented. Once more I wrapped my fictious story around the facts. The combination of both truth and fiction is a very useful tool for an author. I encourage you to use it in your journey as an author at least once.

The Best Things in Life Begin with the Letter B

Paperback ISBN 978-0-9872720-8-9
eBook ISBN 978-0-9872720-7-2

Back Cover Amble:

Curate your 21st Century life with expert guide Aenghus Chisholme as he brings the best things in life into sharp focus. From the everyday, to the unexpected to the ultra-exclusive.

A carefully chosen selection of the very best material and immaterial possessions that may be enjoyed for nothing or obtained with millions of dollars, are laid before you to peruse.

Choose from the superlative belongings that life offers and realise that the best things in life really do begin with the letter 'B'

Author's Notes:

Approximately = 33,000 words.

Writing Time = 3 months. Including, editing and re-writes. One chapter per sitting. Some short, some long. There was no specific word-count for this highly enjoyable exercise in cataloguing a list of things that I enjoy that happen to begin with the letter B

i. Editor:

I must confess, I was the only editor for this one. If you see any obvious boo-boos please write to me and let me know; thanks.

ii. Chapters:

I limited this to 50 chapters. Originally the book was going to be 101 great things that begin with the letter B. But I changed it after about 10 chapters. I edited my original list right down to my top 50, to make it more digestible.

iii. Plot Synopsis:

As with all of my writing, there is the surface story and the underlying one. This appears on the face of it to be a list of things both high-end and free-of-charge that I enjoy. Those things that really do give me joy. However, the underlying tone is a rather serious one. And it is all about consumerism. The point of the entire book being to take a long hard look at what you are filling your life with. If it is just material possessions, then you run the risk of becoming a hoarder. The more you hoard, the more vacuous you will end up feeling.

If in doubt, throw it out. You don't need too many things dragging you down or holding you to ransom. If it is something that you like, then I'm sorry, it's not good enough to be a part of your life. It has to be something that you absolutely love.

iv. Characters:

The characters are the people, places, objects and otherwise that I write about in the book. From Bugatti to the colour blue. Living in Australia, I get to enjoy a blue sky for quite a lot of the year. It costs me precisely nothing. But it is extremely valuable to me. The true value of something cannot really be measured in currency, but only the emotional satisfaction that bestows.

v. The writing process:

It certainly was very different writing in chapters instead of my usual 2000-word count. There was a feeling of a little less discipline than usual to get this book done. Nevertheless, I found it an enjoyable experience. One that I repeated with this book. Chapters, not a word count.

vi. Mistakes:

This was the first book that I put into the new print-on-demand paperback system from Amazon. Oh boy, did I mess up those margins. I could go back and fix them, but I prefer to have them the way that they are to remind me that not everything needs to be perfect in order to be released into the world.

Don't strive for absolute perfection, it simply can never be achieved. And you will just become frustrated attempting to do so.

My subsequent books have been formatted with more precision. I have kept the specifications and just replicate them book after book, easy!

Don't Delay Writing Your Book

Paperback ISBN 978-0-6480789-9-9
eBook ISBN 978-0-6483653-0-3

Back Cover Amble:

Too many of us think that we have a great written work within us, that one day we will sit down and scribe. But that day never comes. Don't be one of those people. Become a writer today!

Self-published author Aenghus Chisholme spells-out in clear steps, how to achieve your goal of writing that story that you've been thinking about for so long.

There are learnings to be discovered from the journey that another has taken. Like a guide in a foreign land, Aenghus will lead you to the very heart of how to produce your first book.

Author's Notes:

Approximately = 17,000 words.

Writing Time = 1 month. Including, editing and re-writes of this version. As stated before, the procedures manual version was abandoned. You could easily add another month for the time taken on that version. For this version I wrote two chapters per writing session.

i. Editor:

I have been the only editor for this book.

ii. Chapters:

28 chapters in total, including the author's notes on my works this far.

iii. Plot Synopsis:

Abandoning the procedures manual style was liberating. I recall when I worked for the facilities management company, I wrote manual after manual. I would often joke with my colleagues that if I wrote 12 chapters of 'Mary had a little lamb" that nobody would notice.

It is incredibly gratifying to write something that I hope will get others out there to finally get going and get writing once and for all.

iv. Characters:

I hope that you see yourself in here somewhere. Because if you do, then there is a chance that I can touch a nerve with you and convince you to shake off the bindings of eternal delay that you are wrapping yourself up in. Get writing now!

v. The writing process:

I felt that I had to get this out quickly before poor old Australia is geo-locked to the AU Amazon site only. Without access to the KDP portal, I will be relegated to Google Play, Smashwords and Xinxii only. I really needed this book more than any other to be available as a paperback. It is the sort of thing that you give to a family member or friend that has been moaning about writing their Magnus Opus Scriptum one day.

vi. Mistakes:

Not doing it sooner! I should have realised that I was doing something that many people dream about, but few actually do. If I had realised the number of people that I could potentially help, I would have done this years ago.

This feels very much like my laser eye surgery. I have worn spectacles since 1980, and pretty much despised them for every year that I had them. Finally, in the year 2005 I had corrective vision laser surgery. Miracle! Why didn't I do it a decade ago? Goodness knows I had had a stable prescription for the last 20 years. I was more than eligible.

If I could turn back time, I would definitely have had it done in the 1990's. But I can't. So, now I am left with exactly the same remorse. This book should have been written probably after my second book. So that a sign-post was planted for others to follow. My apologies for my tardiness. But don't let that become an excuse for you to delay for a second longer. Time for you to start writing right now.

Buddy's Big Adventure (children's illustrated book)

Paperback ISBN 978-0-6483653-1-0
eBook ISBN 978-0-6483653-2-7

Back Cover Amble:

Buddy is a Beagle Cavalier puppy. He lives with his family in Sydney Australia. But one day his family moves away, and he is left behind. He wants to be with them until one day he has a big adventure to an airport and a journey around the world. He arrives in Calgary Canada to discover an amazing new home.

Author's Notes:

Approximately = 1,000 words.

Writing Time = 3 weeks.

i. Editor:

I was the only editor on this book.

ii. Chapters:

30 drawings with pages of some pure text only. Not too much. Certainly not enough to intimidate a young reader.

This was designed to transition young readers from story books to written-word-only, books.

iii. Plot Synopsis:

There is nothing like a true story for a plotline that writes itself. My brother and his family and puppy moved to Canada from Australia. This is the story of how Buddy thought that he may have been left behind. But really wasn't. All is well, that ends well.

iv. Characters:

My eldest brother James. His lovely wife and my sister-in-law Kimberley. And my nephew John and niece Heather. And of course, the irrepressible Buddy.

v. The writing process:

This was written per commissioned drawing. Meaning, that I wrote the plotline and then commissioned the drawings. I had to choose a main drawing from the overall synopsis that I had written. Then the storyline was added back in. A very different experience to any writing job that I had assigned myself before. But that is my goal, to write in as many genres as I can. And experience writing in all of its manifestations.

vi. Mistakes:

None. The gratification of giving my nephew and niece a customised story of a major event in their lives was absolutely priceless. I encourage all uncles out there to do it. Mum's and Dad's too.

The End

Connect with Aenghus Chisholme

Visit my website on www.aenghuschisholme.com

No more delaying – start writing your book!

www.ingramcontent.com/pod-product-compliance
Lightning Source LLC
LaVergne TN
LVHW050936080826
845145LV00004B/1288
* 9 7 8 0 6 4 8 0 7 8 9 9 9 *